Praise for *Guarding the Local Church*

After fifty years of ministry, Dick Iverson is a person who knows how to guard the local church from imbalances, unhealthy ministries, and other spiritual parasites that would drain the health from the local church. Drawing from his life experiences, he gives tools for the pastor to draw from in order to judge those things that could harm the flock. It is not often that you can glean fifty years of wisdom from one book and immediately apply the principles to your local church. I recommend this book highly. All pastors and leaders should read it.

—FRANK DAMAZIO
Senior Pastor, City Bible Church of Portland, Oregon

Every minister of the Gospel should read this message several times a year. This will safeguard your church from the constant winds of strange teachings that blow through our cities. This not only sounds the alarm of warning but also gives steps for keeping a congregation grounded in truth. When this teaching was delivered to a group of ministers at a recent regional gathering, we were all mesmerized by the amazing stories that Pastor Iverson has lived through. These are unforgettable illustrations of doctrinal error and how to avoid them. I have known Brother Dick for nearly 35 years and he just gets better and richer and more accurate with time. This message will save a lot of lives, including your own!

—WENDELL SMITH
Senior Pastor, The City Church of Seattle, Washington

Pastor Iverson has invested his life building leaders and strengthening local churches. He is known, respected, and greatly loved as a spiritual father to many all over the world. His wisdom and insight concerning how to recognize and identify true apostolic and prophetic ministries is invaluable to us in this hour.

—MIKE SERVELLO
Senior Pastor, Mt. Zion Ministries of Utica, New York

It is always good to hear from someone who has lived a few years and logged a few experiences. Dick Iverson has "been there and done that." I have learned so much from him on how to avoid the common pitfalls. I commend him for opening up his life to us and not being afraid to share the good, the bad, and the ugly with us to save us and make us stronger. You can learn two ways. You can learn from your own experiences, which is very expensive. Or you can learn from the experiences of other, which is cheaper by far. As you read this book, I encourage you to learn by the experience of a great father in the faith, Dick Iverson.

—BILL SCHEIDLER
Administrator, Minister's Fellowship International

GUARDING
THE
LOCAL
CHURCH

IDENTIFYING FALSE MINISTRIES

by Dick Iverson

CITYBIBLE
PUBLISHING

Published by City Bible Publishing
9200 NE Fremont • Portland, Oregon   97220
Printed in U.S.A.

City Bible Publishing is a ministry of City Bible Church, and is dedicated
to serving the local church and its leaders through the production and distribution
of quality materials. It is our prayer that these materials, proven in the context of the
local church will equip leaders in exalting the Lord and extending His Kingdom.

For a free catalog of additional resources from City Bible Publishing,
please call 1-800-777-6057

GUARDING THE LOCAL CHURCH

ISBN 1-59383-022-X

First Edition, September 2004
Dick Iverson
All Rights Reserved

Printed in the United States of America

DEDICATION

This book is dedicated to all the true shepherds
and watchmen of the local church who are not hirelings
but are true pastors, laying their lives down for the sheep.

TABLE OF CONTENTS

A WORD FROM
THE AUTHOR

We are living in a day when the church is under attack. Over the last two thousand years, the church has faced many attempts to destroy it and its influence. It has never been the attacks from outside of the church that have been a serious threat because the church was built for war. It is the attacks from within that have been the most dangerous.

The reason that I felt the need to share the message found in this book is that we are entering into times and seasons predicted by Jesus and the Apostle Paul. They both indicated that in the last days false ministries would arise within the church and many would be deceived by them. They indicated that such ministries would get worse and worse.

In an attempt to be politically correct and to avoid naming

names or becoming overly critical, many have been hesitant to speak up. On the one hand, I understand that we do not want to speak ill of others who profess to be believers. On the other hand, I recognize that God has called leaders to be watchmen, shepherds, watchdogs and overseers.

It is of no use to have a watchdog that does not bark. If we are called to guard the flock, then we must be willing to warn God's people of danger on the horizon. God gives leaders special discernment for the purpose of identifying those who would come as "angels of light" but who would bring injury to the plan of God.

Fortunately for us, Satan has very few new tricks. By sharing some of my experiences from the past, I believe that I can avoid alienating present day ministers, and, at the same time, give you some effective keys to identifying and avoiding false ministries.

—DICK IVERSON

CHAPTER ONE

LOOKING BACK

have been in the ministry full time for fifty-five years. I started when I was only nineteen years old (which is way too young)! It is because of this youthful beginning that for the first 10-15 years I made a lot of mistakes. When you have little or no experience and no formal training, mistakes are inevitable. I was a zealous young man trying to make my mark on the world. I had a great heart and a passion to serve the Lord.

But I have found over the years that passion itself is not enough. A love for God and a desire to be used of Him is not enough. Those things in themselves will not keep you from mistakes.

When I say mistakes, I am not talking about sinful behavior. Sin

is knowingly transgressing God's laws. Unfortunately in our igno-
rance we can violate principles in God's word that will bear negative
fruit even when our heart is right and our desires are godly. Sincerity
alone is not enough to ensure that we will reap lasting fruit.

My purpose for writing this book is to share with you some of the
early mistakes that I made, with the goal of helping you to avoid the
same pitfalls. There are two ways that we can learn. We can learn from
our own mistakes, which I have to say is very costly. Or we can learn
from the mistakes of others, which is the less painful way to learn.

I want you to learn from some of my mistakes to save you time
and a certain amount of pain as you walk out your destiny. I also
want to strengthen your hands as leaders in the church to equip you
to be able to identify the signs of false ministries that will do damage
to the work of God in these days.

MY BIG START

As a young man I had the honor of having T. L. Osborn as the senior
pastor of our little church in Portland, Oregon. In those days he was
almost as young as I was. But these were days when God was moving
in powerful ways.

When he started his crusade ministry he asked me to join him
to help with the tent and assist in the services as an attendant. I saw
God move in powerful ways. This was in the late 1940s, a decade
where there was a break out in miracle ministry. As I watched T. L.

night after night something began to stir in me that said, "I would like to do what he is doing!"

After a couple of years T. L. moved his crusade to Jamaica. After watching for those years I was sure that I was now ready to launch out on my own. So at the ripe old age of nineteen, I seized my big opportunity. The main crusades were in the larger cities, but I would go into the more rural areas and take the crusade to them.

So I left the evangelistic party and went out into the bush. That is why I love the Jamaicans so much today, because they are the only ones that would let me preach to them. At age 19 they let me practice on them and that is really where I got my start in the ministry. God did some wonderful things in Jamaica. I could tell many exciting stories of ministry in Jamaica, The Bahamas, and Cuba. It was a season that God let me know that He was for me and that I had a genuine call to preach.

PASTORING WITH MY PARENTS

Shortly after this experience I came back home to that little church. Some big changes had taken place. T. L. Osborn had resigned as pastor to give himself full time to the crusade ministry and my parents were asked to cover the church. In conjunction with that change the church withdrew from its denominational affiliation and became an independent church.

In 1951 my parents now had the responsibility of this small

church. However, my dad was not really a pastor in his gifting. He was a very faithful man, but public ministry ability and the charisma associated with it were lacking. Actually, my mom was more of the preacher even though there was no question that my dad was in charge. For this reason my parents asked Edie and me to co-pastor with them.

For the next ten years Edie and I would go in and out. When we would come home I would do most of the preaching. My dad was clearly in charge, but he enjoyed the help and we were happy to give it.

Those first years were probably the most important years of my life. It was in those years that I really got my training. I still had no real understanding of the local church and the principles that govern it. I still had no real concept of true servant leadership. I had very little when it came to understanding the core values that are dear to me now. It was actually about 15 years before my "core values" would change and become more defined.

MEETING EVERETT PARROT

If you are from my generation you might remember Evangelist Everett Parrot. Everett Parrot was a great evangelist in the 1930s and 1940s. He was a distant relative to Katherine Kuhlman. He shook city after city with his miracle ministry. As a teenager I had heard about him but was never able to attend any of his meetings.

He had a powerful ministry and would pack the auditoriums with those wanting to witness the miracles and the healings that took place in his ministry.

In the 50s when I was co-pastoring the little church in Portland, Everett Parrot walked in our church service one morning. He was in his 80s by this time and his "heyday" was over, but in my mind it was as if Billy Graham had walked into our little church.

Everett Parrot had been out of the crusade ministry for a number of years, but back in the 1930s, and especially in the early 1940s, he was quite famous. We had at the most a hundred people in our church at that time. I was just overwhelmed that Everett Parrot was in our little church. So immediately after the service I welcomed him.

He was a very feeble old man, but I was mesmerized. I fell in love with the man of God who was used long before I was even around. He had brought such blessing. I couldn't believe that I had a "Billy Graham" (I use this as a point of comparison) into our church. I saw him in the spirit. Even though he was very old, very feeble, did not have much fire power left and was in his last days, I saw him as a spiritual giant.

One day he asked me if I would like to visit him at his home in Beaverton, Oregon. He was all by himself since his wife had passed away. I told him that I would be honored to do so.

Shortly after that conversation I drove out to Beaverton and found his very modest two bedroom bungalow. I walked into his living room and I was shocked at what I saw. His home was very poor in its decor. In fact, he had "wallpapered" the entire front room with advertisements of his meetings of 20 years ago. He probably had 150–200 of these clippings around his walls. The clippings were yellow by this time. I had never seen anything like this!

This man had an amazing run of ministry. Crowds! Crowds! Crowds! Here I was in his house. I was honored to be there but I have to say I had a weird feeling. It was all so surreal. I could see he had his little easy chair that he sat in and all that occupied his time was looking at what he had done in past years

Shortly after my visit he passed away. I went to the funeral for this great man of God. I was absolutely shocked. There were seven people there! Seven people! I was grieved. This man had spent a whole lifetime in ministry and was as sincere as a person can be, yet only seven people showed up at his funeral. At the time I said to myself, "This is wrong!" I didn't know what was wrong about it, but I knew something was not quite right.

THE BRITISH ISLE CRUSADES

At that time I still had no biblical "core values" concerning the house of the Lord. I was in and out of the little church in Portland which was more like the home base for my crusade ministry.

Edie and I spent quite a bit of time in England and Ireland in evangelistic and healing crusades. We would fill large city auditoriums. Our gatherings were not in the tens of thousands but for us to have several thousand people was not uncommon. Sometimes we would fill an auditorium twice in one night. I was as sincere then (in my mid 20s) as I am today, but I began to wonder what I was doing. What is this all about?

Because of these experiences I have always had a certain fondness for the British Isles, especially Ireland. Over the years I have grieved when I heard on the news of cities in Northern Ireland such as Armagh, Lurgan, Portadown and Eneskillen being bombed by the I.R.A., because in every one of those places we had rented main auditoriums, put my picture in the newspaper and advertised—"Healing Revival—Bring the Sick." We had prayed for the sick and people got saved. Now there was civil war between Catholics and Protestants with violence and bombings.

In the early 60s, because of my father's health, I had to get more and more involved in the church so the crusade days were behind me. But I was curious. I wondered what it would be like to go back and visit all of the people who had gotten saved under our ministry. I wondered if we could gather a large crowd again. I decided to plan a trip.

LOOKING FOR FRUIT

I went back to the places where I had been with these big crowds. Something was different this time. It wasn't the same. We went back to one place where we had been in those former days where we had rented a wood factory building and, according to the newspapers, there had been 3,500 in attendance. In addition, there had been over 800 conversions with many of those being Catholics.

When we went back to the only auditorium that was available in this place, which would only seat about 400. I knew that this would simply not be big enough. After all, I wanted to visit all "my" converts and friends from the great meetings just a couple of years prior. I figured I would have to push my way through the crowd outside to get to the platform. Because we had personally dealt with over 800 who were saved in those previous meetings we inherently knew that they would be there with their families and friends.

To our amazement, when I arrived to this advertised gathering, the auditorium wasn't even full. I inquired what had happened. Friends explained to me that after I had left, when the crusades were over, the other religious groups put out a lot of anti-Pentecostal tracts saying this miracle crusader and his teaching was "of the devil." As a result there was a lot of confusion and it just literally destroyed the harvest.

I can still remember the hundreds of young people, mostly in their 20s, standing around the front, saying, "We're ready to give our lives to Jesus and really make something count." As they were standing there I would say, "God bless you. God bless you all. Now go to the church of your choice now and serve the Lord. Goodbye! Goodbye! Goodbye!" And I left.

From there I visited more of the places where we had a marvelous move of God and found the same thing to be the case. The great harvest was lost. There was no lasting fruit.

I say this with a heavy heart because for 15 years this is how I had operated. And what did I have to show for it? Something was wrong. Something had to change and I knew that the something that needed changing was me. My core values needed changing. I needed to understand something about the church that Jesus is building.

At this time I didn't understand that Jesus is building "His church." I didn't understand what that meant. And the gates of hell shall not prevail! I thought Jesus was building "my ministry." I thought I was the next Oral Roberts to come on the scene, only I hadn't been discovered yet! I'm serious! I wasn't known in America but I figured it was just a matter of time.

I want to make it clear that I am by no means putting down evangelism and crusade ministry. But I when I was involved in it I worked totally independent of the church. I would come into a community and call the pastors on the phone and say, "I'm Dick Iverson and I am here to hold a meeting in the city auditorium and if you wish to cooperate you are welcome." I believe that my harvest was lost because I was not covered by the local churches of the area.

CHAPTER TWO

THINGS START
TO CHANGE

t was in the mid 60s before my core values began to change. During the first ten years of our church we had two serious splits in this little church of about 100. One evangelist that we had invited in to do a series of meetings split our church. His meetings were so successful he suddenly "got called" to start his own church in our own town. The sad thing is he built right off of our meetings and took half of our church with him.

How could this happen? I am one of God's choice servants. Remember, I was just as sincere then as I am now. However, I did not know how to discern true and false ministry. I could not recognize ministries that had their own personal agenda and not the agenda of the Lord. Part of this is due to the fact that my own understanding of what God is doing and what He is building was so lacking. If you don't have your core values in order, especially concerning the only thing Jesus said He was building, you are going to be vulnerable and you are going to have a lot of problems.

Jesus said in Matthew 16 that He was going to build His Church and the gates of hell would not prevail against it. In other words, the Church is going to succeed. It is going to accomplish God's intended purpose for it. If you are not building what God is building, you are going to waste your life.

Jesus did not say, I will build your ministry and you will be prosperous. He is building His Church. You don't want to waste your life just building your ministry, doing your thing, making a name for yourself, doing wonderful works. If you are only interested in building your ministry you will not get the reward of a good and faithful servant. You may build a good life for yourself in the here and now, but your fruit will not remain and you will lose out on what God has prepared for you in the eternal future.

I want you to think about this. The government of God has been placed in His Church. Is that right? "Obey them that have the rule over you for they must give an account for your souls" (Hebrews 13:17). So if you are not a part of His Church, and you are not building His Church and you are doing anything but building His Church—guess what? You could be actually communicating a spirit of lawlessness in those that you convert. "Look at the evangelist! He doesn't answer to anybody. Why should I answer to anybody?" Do you hear what I'm saying? We must be building what God is building.

There is an old chorus we sing that comes to my mind based on Matthew 16 and the word of Jesus. It goes like this, "Jesus is building His church, Jesus is building His church, and the gates of hell shall not prevail, for Jesus is building his church." That's what it's all about! Did He give the apostle, prophet, pastor, teacher, evangelist so they might be great in His kingdom? No! It was so that they might equip the saints for the work of the ministry (Ephesians 4:11-12)! Now that takes the wind out of our sails if our main goal is to be somebody or to be famous. We are not so hot. But God has given us a charge and it's a wonderful charge. I would never want to do anything but what I've done the last 50 years (after I got past the first fifteen).

I want to share a little bit about those first years. As I said before, I co-pastored with my father for the first ten years, from 1951–1961, before taking the senior role in 1961. During those first ten years I was the principle speaker and very active in the church. But we had two major church splits. We had an evangelist with a sign gift ministry who held meetings for several weeks. It was miraculous. He could point people out and call their name and addresses, the name of their doctor, etc. Goose bumps were on the goose bumps! After several weeks he went across town and immediately rented an auditorium and took half the people with him. Well, I look back and say, "Thank you Lord," because I learned an awful lot right then. I feel part of my job, as a spiritual overseer to you as leaders, is to share with you what I have learned.

CHAPTER THREE

THE CHALLENGE OF
THE SCRIPTURES

n the opening chapters of the book of Revelation we find the exalted Jesus ministering as the Great High Priest to the seven churches of Asia. The church at Ephesus was one of the great churches. The Book of Ephesians is one my favorite books of the Bible. If you want to know God's master plan, God's overview, just study Ephesians and you will see the picture very clearly.

This was a great church but it had some problems (Rev. 2:1–7). They had left their first love. That was a problem. They got so used to the routines and the program of the church that they forgot what it was all about. They forgot that it was all about Him. They had a lot of things going for them for which Jesus had good things to say. He said, "*I know your works, your labor, your patience, and that you cannot bear those who are evil. And you have tested those who say they are apostles and are not, and have found them liars.*"

When I was reading this account the other day and read the words, "you have tested those who say they are apostles and are not," it just jumped out at me. I felt as if the Lord spoke to me and said, "How do you test ministries?" I replied, "Lord I am not really sure." And then He said to me," "Well, check the Bible." I immediately thought, "What a good idea!"

Jesus said it was alright to test ministries; in fact, He commended them for doing so. Just because someone calls themselves an apostle, it does not mean that they are in fact an apostle.

We are living in a time when we are seeing a restoration of true apostolic and prophetic ministries. It is a wonderful thing and it is part of God's overall plan to see these ministries fully released and functioning in the days prior to His return. But the Scriptures also give us ample warning that not everyone who claims to be a true prophet is a true prophet. Not everyone who calls themselves an apostle is an apostle in God's eyes.

The last days will be characterized by deception. There will be many false ministries. It will not be easy to tell the difference at times. The church at Ephesus had figured out a way to test these ministries and they had determined that some of them who claimed to be true ministries were liars. Jesus said to them, "*You tested those that are apostles and that are not and found them liars.*"

In Acts 20:28-31, Paul talks to this very same church. He called for the elders at the church of Ephesus and gathered them together and said to them,

> *Therefore take heed to yourselves and to all the flock, among which the Holy Spirit has made you overseers, to shepherd the church of God which He purchased with His own blood. For I know this, that after my departure savage wolves will come in among you, not sparing the flock. Also from among yourselves men will rise up, speaking perverse things, to draw away the disciples after themselves. Therefore watch, and remember that for three years I did not cease to warn everyone night and day with tears.*

Paul instructed them first of all to "*take heed to yourselves.*" He is really giving them some strong words. The first steps in judging ministry is to judge ourselves. We have to make sure we take the beam out of our own eye so that we can see clearly. We also have to be constantly on guard so that the things that form a seed bed for becoming a false ministry are not in our own hearts.

Paul further warns them, "*Also from among yourselves, men will raise up speaking perverse things to draw away disciples after themselves. Therefore watch, and remember that for three years I did not cease to warn everyone night and day with tears.*" He says that wolves will come in from the outside and wolves will come from the inside.

Why do you suppose God called His leaders watchmen? In Isaiah 56:10, God speaks through the prophet and points out a condition that is not good for the people of God. The watchmen are not being what they are supposed to be. God said,

> *His watchmen are blind, they are all ignorant; they are all dumb dogs, they cannot bark; sleeping, lying down, loving to slumber. Yes, they are greedy dogs which never have enough. And they are shepherds who cannot understand; they all look to their own way, every one for his own gain, from his own territory. "Come," one says, "I will bring wine, and we will fill ourselves with intoxicating drink; tomorrow will be as today, and much more abundant.*

He called the watchmen "blind, ignorant, dumb dogs who cannot bark." Have you ever gone up to a house with a ferocious dog sitting on the front porch? He growls as you approach and your heart begins to beat faster. But as you approach the steps and get closer to him you realize that he is "all bark and no bite." You see that his tail is wagging. The dumb guard-dog might just as well be saying "Go ahead, come on in! Everything is fine. Go ahead and spoil all my master's goods." Dumb dog! Doesn't he know that I could be a burglar!

The Lord uses these illustrations to help us understand our job. He calls leaders to be overseers. They are a bishop. That is their job. He calls leaders shepherds. Why did He use those terms? Watchman, watchdog, bishop, shepherd! The shepherd has a rod and a staff. One is to grab hold of the neck of the sheep that is wandering and pull him back in the flock and the other one is to hit that wolf over the head to protect the flock. That is a leader's job. The leader's job is to protect the sheep and preserve the local church!

CHAPTER FOUR

WILLIAM BRANHAM— TRUE OR FALSE?

n 1948 William Branham came to our city and literally turned my pastor and my life around. My pastor was T. L. Osborn, who was just six years older than me. We attended that meeting and we saw things that we had never seen before. It was like the New Testament came alive. Let me share something that happened in that meeting which is recorded in William Branham's life story.

T. L. and I sat together in the civic auditorium in Portland. There were 3500 people in attendance and we were seated in the balcony. Just as Brother Branham came to the podium, a big, gruff guy walked down the aisle. I was rather surprised as I watched him come down. Everyone was looking at him and wondering what he would do.

As he walked up to the platform a security man stepped out and stopped him. Brother Branham saw the man and said, "Let him come." The scene that unfolded was reminiscent of David and Goliath because Branham was about 5'5" and this guy was probably 6'5". The man began to say, "You're a fake! And I am going to knock you down and take you out." Branham quietly replied, "What do you want?" The man's answer was, "You're a phony. I'm gonna take you out." The scene was serious. The people in the congregation were getting extremely nervous especially when the man raised his fists for action.

I didn't know this at the time but I found out later that this same man had broken up a lot of missions down in the Portland area by literally knocking ministers down. However, I was scared for Brother Branham because he was my hero. He was my hero because for the first time in my life I had watched a person pray for a deaf and dumb child who had never heard and saw an instant miracle. It was so impacting that I was crying like a baby. Now I am sitting there and my hero is getting ready to be whipped and I am scared.

Brother Branham kept saying, "What do you want?" in a very kind manner. "You are a phony, a fake, a snake in the grass!" the man would reply. If you have ever read Brother Branham's book he shares that at times the spirit of the Lord would come upon him and he would feel the angel of the Lord like a whirlwind. It wasn't anything anyone could see, but it was very real to him.

My heart was pounding! Here is my hero and he is about to get leveled. Finally he turned to the audience and, after he had felt this anointing come on him, Branham said, "Would everybody just bow their heads? This man has defied the servant of God and he must bow down before me. Please bow your heads."

Well, I bowed my head and put my hands over my face, but my fingers were spread and my eyes were open! I was sitting in the balcony and had a great view. I wasn't going to miss this one! Brother Branham turned and said, "In Jesus Name, bow down." "I'll bow down to nobody," the man retorted. Branham repeated softly, "In Jesus name, bow down." "I will not bow down to anybody," the man insisted. He was becoming very belligerent. Suddenly it was like an invisible hand came down from on the top of this big guy pushing him down. You could see he was fighting. Brother Branham said it three times, "bow down in Jesus' name." This big guy started slowly going down even though he was trying not to. It was like something was pushing him down until he was on his knees and finally, on his face. There he was on the floor at the feet of Brother Branham.

Can you imagine how that would affect you as an 18 year old? Jesus you are real! I'm ready to go!

After a period of time, the man slowly got up. Actually he sort of backed up like a dog on his fours as if to say, "What hit me?" He looked around. Brother Branham was exhorting the congregation saying, "Only believe, all things are possible, just trust God." The man continued to back up. Finally, I watched him run down the aisle. He had his coat on the backseat and he grabbed it as he ran out. Of course, everyone clapped.

A LATER ENCOUNTER

Years later, in 1961, William Branham was in Salem, Oregon and, again, I was all excited. My hero was back in the area. I was in ministry because of that impact of the supernatural. I am now the pastor of "Deliverance Temple" and meeting in a theatre that seated 650 people even though our attendance was still just 100. Nothing was really happening yet. But I am excited to see my hero.

Let me intersperse here that Ern Baxter traveled with William Branham for many years. The reason he traveled with him was because Brother Branham had very little theological training. I don't say that disparagingly. He just never had any real training in the Bible. So Ern Baxter would travel with him and he would teach before Branham would take the platform. I remember when he was teaching wishing that he would quit so that the man of power could do his work. But Ern Baxter was a great Bible teacher and he would put the word on the people. After several years they separated and no longer traveled together.

On this night I walked into the auditorium that was reasonably full with maybe a thousand people, so excited to hear my hero. Remember, I do not have my cores values straight at this time. That night I heard him say, "God is through with the church!" He took that scripture out of Revelation about the Laodicean church. "He has vomited the church out of his mouth. He is now speaking through His messenger." I began to feel funny. Something wasn't right. Now remember, I want to believe Brother Branham. I really want to believe him. He is my hero. He was preaching on legalism and dress and everything you could imagine. "The church is Jezebel," he would say.

Before I continue, let me add this. We all know there is an "apostate" church that is vomited out of God's mouth. The Bible talks about the false church in I Timothy 3. But when you make those kinds of statements and say, "God is through with his church" you need to be careful. If the church is Christ's wife, and it is, you best be careful what you say about her. Now, we know the church is not perfect. Ephesians 5:27 tells us that He is going to come for a perfect or glorious church without spot or wrinkle. She has a few spots now and we all know that. We know that the church is not perfected and that this is what we are here for, to help bring her to maturity.

But Branham made this blanket statement a number of times, "God is through with his church. He is now speaking through the messenger. He no longer speaks to the church." And I kept thinking to myself, "Wait a minute! Jesus loves the church and He gave Himself for it. Where does it say He quit loving the church?" God loves His body. He will always love His body. The church is the body of Christ.

If God didn't love the church, He would have had plenty of excuses to get rid of the Corinthian church fast. It was so blemished and mangled with extreme problems. You and I would have put "Ichabod" over the door. He didn't. He sent Paul and brought them into correction. There was immorality, they were suing one another, they abused the table of the Lord, they were devouring each other and backbiting, but He kept working on her.

I remember leaving the meeting that night deeply troubled in my spirit. I did not have my core values yet, but something was starting to churn inside. I had experienced the loss of a harvest in the evangelistic field, and now am I to believe that God is no longer speaking to His church?

A SUDDEN END

Brother Branham believed that he was Elijah and that he was the last messenger. Less than a year after that meeting in Salem, he was driving down a freeway in Arizona when a drunk driver veered across two lanes of freeway and hit him head on. He was killed immediately—a violent and horrible death.

His followers were so convinced that he was indeed Elijah that they did not accept his death. They kept his body on ice for weeks believing that he would be resurrected. Even today there are Branhamites in the world. They still listen to all of his tapes and they still believe that one day he will return and restore all things.

Now, I am not the judge, but I often wondered why God took him out so quickly and in that way. I can only say that I think God wanted to remove him because he had become a distraction to the purposes of God. You might say that it "just happened." No, I think otherwise. I think when you touch the wife of Jesus, the heavenly husband, He is not just going to sit back. You can walk up to me if you want to and slap me and kick me and say "I don't like you Dick and I wish you had never been born." And I would reply, "Well, that's the way it goes." But if you go over and slap or kick my wife, you will never touch her again unless it is over my dead body, because a husband has something in him that will not allow it.

I am not putting Brother Branham down. He was a man of God. He got into error and false teaching. It doesn't mean he didn't go to heaven. I think William Branham is in heaven, but how much better it could have been.

I am having all of these experiences and slowly my core values were beginning to evolve.

CHAPTER FIVE

WHY SATAN ATTACKS THE CHURCH

ave you ever wondered why the church has been under vicious attack from its very inception at the day of Pentecost? Charlatans, con men and false teachers have tried to misuse it and abuse it for their own ends continually over the past two thousand years. I have been in the ministry fifty-five years and I have watched the devastation of so many local churches. I have seen leaders fall and their churches scattered. I have seen men rise up and smite the shepherd and scatter the sheep. I often watched (with my heart broken) and seen great churches disintegrate through internal strife over such inane and foolish things as the color of the carpet. It seems like Satan has aimed his heaviest artillery against the church since the day of its conception. Why do you suppose that is true? Why is Satan so bent on the total annihilation of every local church?

SATAN'S REVENGE

Let me use this illustration. Suppose you had a bitter enemy and this enemy hated you with a passion. But every time he came against you, you would defeat him. You would overcome him. You would so hurt him and destroy his works against you that he was continually put to open shame and you would spoil him in front of principalities and powers. You made an open triumph over him, even to the tearing away of all the authority and power that he had.

If you were that enemy and that happened to you, how would you get even with that person who totally conquered and stripped you of the keys of death and hell and all authority and power? How would you get even with the one who had made you a laughing stock? Let me tell you what has been happening the past two thousand years.

According to Ephesians 5, Christ and the Church are related the same way that a husband and wife are. It is also clear from this same passage that Jesus loved the Church so much that He gave Himself for it and that the Church is so united with Him that it is considered part of His flesh and bone. The Church is so joined with Christ that He uses marriage as an illustration of the bond between them—"for the two shall become one flesh. This is a great mystery, but I speak concerning Christ and the church" (Eph. 5:31-32).

THE BRIDE OF CHRIST

Now if you were my enemy, and you knew from experience that you could not be victorious against me, what would you do? You would come after those things that you knew were important to me. You would strike at my wife and my family. You would do everything you could to hurt me by attacking my wife and my children.

At the same time, if you were my enemy, you could come against me personally, be abusive to me personally, and you could hurt me personally and you would have a better chance of getting away with it than if you would strike my wife. If you came against my wife and leveled an attack against her you would feel my full wrath. Only over my dead body would you hit her again.

I believe that this is why the church is under constant attack and why God put shepherds, watchmen, watchdogs, overseers, to protect her from all of the false ministries that are arrayed against her. The Church is the apple of God's eye. It is the bride of Christ. It is His inheritance and He is jealous over it with a godly jealously. He wants us to share that same passion for the Church.

Having a passion for the Church is not a mystical thing. Having a passion for the Church translates itself into having a passion for each local church. It means being jealous over each local congregation of believers that no one destroy the work of God in that place. It means taking up the shepherd's mantle and the shepherd's rod and protecting the church from those who would seek to abuse churches for their own ends. At times this actually means exposing and confronting false ministries or "wolves in sheep's clothing."

CHAPTER SIX

LEARNING BY MORE EXPERIENCES

During those first fifteen years of pastoring I had many experiences that caused me to wake up and "smell the coffee." All through each of these God was trying to get through to me as a pastor and leader.

One man in our city had gained prominence as the head of the Full Gospel Business Men in Portland. He was a very wealthy man who for the purpose of this story I will name "Fred." Fred enjoyed the spiritual platform that he was given through his work with the FGB organization. Soon he began to have prayer meetings in his home on

Friday evenings. He was a very dominant man who had a rather demonstrative ministry in the area of deliverance. This fit well with our local church at the time which was named "Deliverance Temple."

Many of our people, especially those who did not feel that we were doing enough in the area of deliverance, began to attend his meetings until over half of our people were going to the Friday night prayer meetings at his house. I didn't think too much about it (remember, my core values weren't together yet). They were getting blessed and that was great. But I kept getting reports back from those who had been in the meeting saying that he had cast out a lot of "sex demon." It seemed that all of the demons that he was dealing with were somehow "sex" related (e.g. lust demons, immoral demons, etc.). I began thinking that it was kind of weird—only sex demons.

One Sunday evening in the early 60s we had a visiting speaker at our church. As the speaker came up to the pulpit he looked out to the congregation and saw that another young evangelist, whom we will call Thomas, was in the audience. The visiting minister did a very unethical thing and said, "You know, I don't really have the message and I see young Thomas here tonight. I believe he has the message."

I was sitting on the platform but he didn't even consult with me and ask if he could turn the pulpit over to this young ministry. I thought it was kind of strange. What was I supposed to do? Was I to make a big scene and blurt out, "No, he doesn't!" (By the way, today I would do just that!) So young Thomas preached that night.

He did a good job and preached a normal message. After the service was over the young preacher went out with some young people. He was a single young man and so I did not think anything about him going out with the other singles.

Not long after this incident I received a call from Fred, the Full Gospel Businessmen leader. "You'd better get over here pastor because I've have one of your young people over here who has confessed to having had an "affair" with Thomas, the young evangelist."

I was horrified! The girl in question was a brand new convert whose name was Sue (not her real name). I was sick inside. I rushed to his home and before I could even begin to work with the situation he said, "God showed me that the young evangelist is going up and down the West Coast seducing women in churches. God showed me. I didn't even have to see him to know this. He came into your church and you let him in the pulpit to seduce the people. And now he has had an affair with this young lady."

To be honest, at this time I was not concerned about defending myself and my reputation or discussing the incident of the pulpit. I was worried about Sue. So I went over and sat down by her to pray with her, comfort her and do the best I could to ensure her that God would forgive her, heal her and restore her.

Fred was more concerned with rebuking me as a pastor. While I was trying to minister peace to Sue, he couldn't stop going on about what he perceived had taken place. He kept telling me how God showed him what a poor pastor I was in not discerning this wolf among the sheep. Remember, I had not asked Evangelist Thomas to preach. Fred, however, did not want to be confused with facts. As far as he was concerned I was a bad pastor and unfit for the ministry. He would use this in his own mind to justify his drawing people to himself as a sort of "rescuer" of those under my care.

I still was unsure about what was happening in all of this. I knew that I eventually needed to confront the evangelist. My first concern, however, was to make sure Sue was going to be alright and that she would remain strong in her new found faith.

About two weeks later Sue slipped up along side me at a prayer meeting and said, "You know, pastor, I think you've got the wrong impression." I said, "What do you mean?" "Nothing really happened. He kissed me and said he would write to me, but that was all that happened." "You mean you didn't have an affair?"

Now you know when you use the word "affair" in regard to two single young people, you would think the worst and I did think the worst. Now she was saying "He kissed me and that is all." He had told her he would write to her and she hadn't heard from him in a number of weeks so she went to the prayer meeting and told Fred that Thomas said that he loved her and was interested in her. He immediately read into it that she had an affair of fornication.

So, I called Fred up on the phone and said, "Fred, you have misunderstood. Sue was not involved sexually with this young evangelist. He kissed her and said he would write to her and never wrote to her." He replied, "Don't you tell me that he didn't have a sexual relationship. God doesn't play 'tidily winks' with me."

By this time Fred had already been using this incident as a testimony at the Full Gospel Business Men meetings. He had actually been speaking against our church and our leadership and he was ranking us down. I had heard about this so I said to him, "Please don't use that testimony again because I believe her that she didn't have a sexual relationship."

ANOTHER INCIDENT

About the same time a teenager in our church (I will call her Joyce) began going to Fred's prayer meetings. This young lady soon became another victim of Fred's deliverance ministry. He soon discerned that she had demons of lust in her. With the help of others in the group they began to cast out these lust demons from her, even wrestling her to the floor in the process.

After this incident, Fred developed a special relationship with Joyce as one of his success stories. He invited her to live at his very lovely home. This young girl had come from a very poor home and she rather enjoyed the luxury of her new lifestyle. His primary interest in her was to take her around to all the Full Gospel Business Men's meetings to give her testimony indicating how she was delivered from these demons. As her pastor, I was very concerned. I had received a report that she had become the object of several "deliverance" sessions in the Friday night meetings. In fact, it was reported that they had to keep delivering her to make it interesting so they would wrestle with her and hold her down.

Joyce had always been such a bright young lady and to think of her with all this demonic activity did not register with me. Finally, I brought her into my office one day and said, "Joyce, I don't think you are demon possessed. What's going on?" She hung her head. Soon she began to cry. She said, "You're right, pastor. I know it. But I've got so much attention since I have been going to those meetings and I can live in this beautiful home and travel and be in banquets."

When I heard this I was upset. So I called Fred up again and said, "Listen, Joyce is not coming back to any of your meetings ever again. She was not demon possessed. She is a godly person raised up in our church. Please don't use that testimony."

Fred and I were beginning to develop quite a relationship. He got very angry with me again. He again reminded me that God does not play "tidily winks" with him and that he had rightfully discerned those spirits. Who did I think I was to question his gift? I was just a lowly pastor of a small insignificant church.

A SLOW LEARNER

Let me share the third case with you. I am a slow learner! A young girl from our church (whom I will call Mary), who was a little overweight, stopped by Fred's home one day. She asked him to pray with her because she wanted to have a boyfriend. He immediately began to discern "demons of lust" in her and told her that God showed him that she was going to be a prostitute. And with that he sent her home. She was from our church! Mary was so devastated by Fred's prognostication that she went home immediately, took a razor blade and slit her wrists to take her life, because if she was going to be a prostitute she wanted to die right then. Thank God, help got to her before she died!

PASTORAL CONFRONTATION

I felt like Popeye the sailor man. That was all I could stand and I could not stand any more. This time I did not call. I went to his door! I told him that I would be announcing from the platform the very next Sunday that no one from our church was to attend the prayer meetings at his home again.

Of course, he got very angry with me. I just let him know that I was notifying him in advance what I was going to do so that when the news came back to him and his meetings dropped off a little he would know what had happened. The next Sunday I did just that. I stood up in front of the congregation and told the congregation that if they were part of our church that they were no longer to attend Fred's prayer meetings. We lost one family over it as a result, but it could have been so much worse since half of the church had been attending his meetings.

Fred went from bad to worse. After the confrontation with me, he began going around publicly saying that God had shown him that there were demonic snakes crawling in and out of the Sunday School rooms of Deliverance Temple biting people and transmitting a spirit of homosexuality to those bitten in our church. There was really nothing that I could do about Fred. He had no covering. The Full Gospel Businessmen was not structured with accountability and discipline in mind. But I could take care of my sheep.

One day, not too long after that, a phone call came telling me that Fred was suffering from leukemia and was not expected to live. I started feeling bad because by this time we had had some "head on" encounters and sharp words. So I called him on the phone to see if I could come over and see him. His reply was, "If you think you are coming over here to pray for me that God is going to heal me, I want you to know that God has already told me that He is going to heal me and raise me up to have a testimony that is going to shake this whole community. Don't bother." I was grieved. That is exactly what he said.

Well, he continued to get worse and worse until finally when he would roll over in bed his bones would break because they were so brittle. Just a short time later he died.

COINCIDENCE OR JUDGMENT

The seemingly premature deaths of both Brother Branham and this brother made me wonder a lot. What happened? Why did my hero die such a violent death? Why did this man in our city who got into such heavy demonology die such a premature and painful death?

The Lord spoke to me. "If Deliverance Temple is the body of Christ and someone attacks the church, which is the body of Christ, look out because I'm not going to let him get away with it." Now, that put the fear of God into me and it was those situations that caused me to begin to search. What is this thing called the local church? What is my call in relationship to it? What is my job as a pastor-protector of the flock?

UNDERSTANDING THE CHURCH

Through all of these early experiences, God was shaping my understanding. What is this thing called "the church" all about? The church is mentioned 114 times in the New Testament. The more I read and the more I meditated on it, eventually the penny dropped. That's what it is all about. It is the body of Jesus. It is the visible expression of Christ in a community. I am not the body of Christ. I am a "member" of the body of Christ. Corporately we make up the body of Christ. Individually (I Corinthians 12) we are but one member. I can't get along without you. You can't get along without me. We need every member of my body of Christ.

It's when my eyes were opened to this revelation that my life was changed. I look back and I see all the foolishness in the way we did things in the church. I was so sincere at the time. I was just as sincere then as I am now. I had sincerity, but it was not coupled with the truth.

You know, if you drink poison you can be as sincere as you want, but it will still kill you. I remember time and time again with my sincerity, I would bring in the best preachers that the nation had to offer. Some may not understand this today, but in that day many of us Pentecostals had a revival center concept (e.g. Seattle Revival Center, Deliverance Temple, San Francisco Revival Center, etc). We all had tried to get the largest building that we could get and invite in the great preachers. Many of these preachers of the 1950s would come through on a circuit from one center to the next. Our church was on the circuit because we had a good sized building for that day. We were excited to have all these evangelists with their magazines and their own personal promotion because they would fill that building. One year we had a dozen different preachers come through, each averaging three weeks of meetings. They would preach every night of the week. Each one had their specialty or their "claim to fame."

When I look back I am ashamed of some of the things that were done in the name of the anointing. I would have to say that there were only two out of those twelve that I would ever allow back in the pulpit. Most of them were nothing more than con artists. Many of them were later proven to be were immoral. Often all they were after was money. Everything you could imagine took place. One man had a red cross appear across his forehead while he was preaching. Of course, when that appeared, people just went bananas. They would proclaim, "God is in the house!"

My desire is not to just be negative but sometimes you have to look at the negatives to know what to do right and avoid the pitfalls. I remember talking to the pastor of the Seattle Revival Center, who had taken the church from his father at the same time I took our church from my father. We were chatting one day and he said, "I am so sick and tired of bringing all these phonies into the church, like these people that have crosses appear on their heads."

He was making reference to a particular minister of that day that was know to have a red cross appear on his forehead while he was preaching. This would always raise the faith level of the people and bring great excitement. I had recently had him in my church. (When I advertised his meetings, by the way, I did not mention anything about the cross appearing and, coincidentally, it never showed up when the guy was at our church. I thought after the meeting was over that it must have been my unbelief because the supernatural sign didn't show up.) I said, "Tell me about it! What do you mean the cross appears? Isn't that God?" "Oh, don't be silly," was his reply. "There's a chemical he puts on his forehead in the shape of a cross and when he preaches his body temperature rises and the chemical make the cross turn red." (Now, don't ask what the chemical is!)

As you can see, I went through many learning experiences.

CHAPTER SEVEN

SATAN'S ATTACK

The verse, I John 4:1-3, helps us understand the relationship that we are to have with Christ:

Beloved, do not believe every spirit, but test the spirits, whether they are of God; because many false prophets have gone out into the world. By this you know the Spirit of God: Every spirit that confesses that Jesus Christ has come in the flesh is of God, and every spirit that does not confess that Jesus Christ has come in the flesh is not of God. And this is the spirit of the Antichrist, which you have heard was coming, and is now already in the world.

This scripture should enlighten us as to who we are in Christ. We are flesh of His flesh, bone of His bone. This is as joined as you can be to Christ, who is our heavenly husband.

In Matthew 7:22-23, Jesus made a very interesting statement. He said, *Many will say to Me in that day, "Lord, Lord, have we not prophesied in Your name, cast out demons in Your name, and done many wonders in Your name?" And then I will declare to them, "I never knew you; depart from Me, you who practice lawlessness!"*

I find it interesting that the Lord does not say that these individuals did not cast out devils and prophesy in His name, and do wonderful works. He simply said, "I never knew you." The term that Jesus used here is the term used for an intimate relationship between a husband and wife. "I never knew you."

How does one have an intimate relationship with Jesus Christ? The only way one can have that type of intimacy is by being a part of His church, which is His wife.

Let me make the following bold statement. *Any ministry or person that hurts, hinders or belittles the local church, the body of Christ, is demonically inspired.* Now, that's heavy. Think about it. Any ministry or person that hurts, hinders or belittles the body of Christ, the local church is demonically inspired.   CRAFTS

There are many ministries that we would most likely see as valid ministries because of the spiritual gifts that operate in their lives. They prophesy, they work wonders and they preach mighty sermons. However, many of these same ministries are not rightly related to a local church. Because of this the net result of their ministry can actually be hindering what God is trying to do and hindering the people that follow them from making the same needed commitment to a local church. Are these true ministries or false ministries?

Rover ?

A HERO OR A CRIMINAL

Let me give you an illustration. In the one hand someone might say, "But you don't know, that prophecy was correct and it changed my life." However, on the other hand, in another situation that same minister may give another prophecy that destroys a life. Please remember that I believe in the prophetic, it is a major ministry in our local church. It is one of our core values.

But let me paint this scenario for you. Let's suppose that we are standing out on a busy street and a man goes to step off the curb to cross the street. He is from another country and is not looking the right way to see the oncoming traffic. Unfortunately, a truck is coming, he is on the verge of being hit, but I grab him a save him. If I saved this man from certain death, what am I? I'm a hero!

The next day there is another situation and a similar person doesn't see a car coming and I tackle him and roll him out of the way. In this case, what am I? I'm a hero!

The third day there is another man patiently waiting for traffic to pass so he can cross the street and I shove him in front of a truck and he is killed. What am I now? Now I am a criminal! A murderer!

Just because a minister is accurate a certain percentage of the time does not make them a valid minister. A false ministry is not false all of the time otherwise there would be no need for discernment. There would be no need to judge apostles. God hates mixture. Now let me qualify this. I realize that we all are susceptible to error. Even in the early church Paul instructed the church to judge prophecy (I Corinthians 14). The reason is that we are all still human vessels.

I am talking about rendering judgment as a pastor and leaders. You are the watchman! As such we must help our people to discriminate when it comes to ministries. There are ministries that build or edify the church and there are those whose fruit is negative in relation to the church. We cannot be afraid to be fruit inspectors. Even Balaam had an accurate prophecy. But the net result of his ministry was to draw the people of God away from a proper commitment to the purposes of God.

SIXTY PERCENT ACCURACY

I have so many illustrations I could give, but one more will suffice to make my point. Several years ago I invited a brother who is very well known nationally to minister upon a strong recommendation from someone that I respected highly. He was a man who operated in a strong "word of knowledge" ministry. I was a little nervous about having him in the first place, because my own early experience had made me somewhat cautious. But to make matters worse, after I had already invited him I got a call from a friend telling me that his "word of knowledge" was very accurate but his "predictions" were about 40 percent wrong.

My friend said that he was very accurate with the initial word. Without any knowledge of who was at a service he would call someone's name, give their address or their doctor's name, etc. From there he would bring the person up, pray for them and often predict an outcome. He said that in his church in one of the services that this evangelist predicted that two people would live and they both died the next week. My friend had to bury them and try to pastor the people through this apparent contradiction.

Because all the arrangements had been made and I had announced his coming, he did, in fact, come to our church. However, because I was the watchman on the wall who was tasked by Jesus to protect the flock, I knew that I needed to go to work. The night before he was to minister I sat down with him and asked some hard questions. I wanted to know why many of his predictions were not correct since his word of knowledge was so accurate.

When I asked him why his predictions were not accurate his response was that whether they come to pass or not is up to the people. If the people don't believe and they die, well, that's their problem. I said, "Wait a minute. I bring my little baby to you and you pray for the baby and you say the baby will live and the baby dies a few days later. It's my fault and the rest of my life I have to live with the fact that if I had faith my baby would be here. Are you going to put that on me?" "Oh, I didn't mean that" he quickly came back. "You said it's not God's problem and it's not your problem so it has to be the fault of the people being ministered to."

We've spent about two hours together on Saturday night, he is supposed to be starting his ministry on Sunday morning, and he is getting a little irritated with me by now because I am confronting him. That's my job! If I do not confront the man, who else will do it? I find that often pastors are intimidated by the gift in such a minister and they just let things slide. Unfortunately many ministries like this have no real covering and no one who holds them accountable. As a result they continue to commit the same mistakes and the real losers are the "people of God."

Suddenly (after two hours of this) he said, "I see what I'm doing." I appreciated his integrity. He said, "I get excited when God gives me a word for somebody. I really do. I get just as excited as the people. I bring them up and tell them the names of their kids. But I want to excite them even more so I predict." I asked him further, "What is the purpose of the world of knowledge?" I said, "I believe that it is to let people know that God knows them. It raises faith. It's a wonderful gift. You do not need to predict, let their faith take them to the next level."

I asked him not to predict anything when he ministered in our church this next day and he agreed. "Call them out. Pray for them, but leave them in the hands of God. Don't predict." It was interesting. He was calling people out and did a good job bringing them up and praying for them. He called out a lady by name who had cancer and brought her forward. She was going to the doctor the next day. He prayed for her. After he prayed he said, "And tomorrow" (he paused and looked at me out of the corner of his eye) "...God will be with you." Then he looked back over at me and winked. It was kind of humorous.

The interest thing is that she went to the doctor the next day and they couldn't find the cancer. But, he didn't have to predict that. I appreciated the fact that he came under authority and didn't predict. It is very important that you are the watchman.

CHAPTER EIGHT

ECCLESIOLOGY

Ecclesiology. Do you know what that is? It's a nice big word! It means the theology of the church. Your ecclesiology is so important in this day. Your understanding of the church determines your treatment of the church.

In my earlier days I didn't have a high value for the house of God. I didn't hate the church members but I didn't understand what I was doing. So, to me the church was like a club. You want to join it? Join it.

My dad used to say this and I said it too. This is only a fellowship. There is nothing here you can belong to. The door swings both ways. Well, guess what the people did? One person came in the front and another one went out the back. For 15 years we never grew because there was "nothing here to belong to." We used to say that we were a filling station. You get tanked up here and then you leave.

A MATTER OF VALUES

Your value of the church determines your treatment of it. I like to use this illustration. Let's say that I find a rather ordinary looking stone outside on the ground in an open field. I pick it up and say, "Wow, that's a beautiful stone. Pastor, look at this stone." And the pastor says politely (to humor me a bit because he actually sees no beauty in it), "Yes, that's nice." Then I shock him further by saying, "Listen I want you to have it. I just found it out here in your field." I force him to take it. He puts it in his pocket and tries to forget all about it.

A few months later right in the same area they discover raw diamonds that are worth a lot of money, some of them right on the surface of the ground. It turns out that they are some of the largest uncut diamonds that have ever been found. They find them right in the same area from which I gave you that "rather ordinary look-ing stone."

Suddenly the pastor thinks to himself, "You know, that stone Dick gave me was kind of unusual. Could it have been? What was I wearing that day?" Immediately he goes to his closet and goes through all of his clothes until he finds the stone in one of his pockets. And sure enough it turns out to be a diamond in the rough. It is worth $200,000 dollars as is.

Let me ask you. How would he treat that "rather ordinary looking stone" now? Well, you can't even begin to compare the church with a $200,000 diamond. One of those people in your church is worth the whole world and God has given you the privilege to watch over that diamond. What a privilege to be an overseer, guardian and shepherd. If you don't understand the importance of that, you are in big trouble because you are not going to treat it right.

Now I know there are problems with every local church. But the church is the apple of God's eye and He sees it as worthy of the life of the Son of God. The value of something is measured by what someone will pay for it. God paid the highest price that could be paid for the church. He bought it with the precious blood of His own dear Son.

CHAPTER NINE

DISCONNECTED MINISTERS

n the church world today there are many leaders, preachers, evangelists, apostles, teachers and prophets that are disconnected from a local church and are in love with their ministry rather than the house of God. They are going about doing wonderful works, because the gifts and callings of God in their lives, but they don't have an intimate relationship with Jesus.

I Corinthians 11:30 is a very familiar passage of scripture, but do we understand it? I Corinthians 11:30 states, *"For this reason*

many are weak and sick among you, and many sleep [die prematurely]."
What reason was Paul speaking about? He stated the reason very
clearly when he said that it was the result of not "discerning the
Lord's body."

Evidently some individuals did not understand that the church
is in fact the spiritual Body of Christ and that our relationship to
it is critical to our well-being as believers. The purpose of our gifts
and ministries is not for our own enrichment or our own sense of
fulfillment, but we are given these gifts to build what God is building which is the House of the Lord—the Church. We are not just
serving our ministry, we are serving the House of the Lord, and all
true ministry must build the House of God if we want our heavenly
husband's approval.

I Corinthians 12 is one of the most powerful passages of scripture to explain how the church functions. In this passage, which is
clearly focused on the local church, not the universal church, it
tells us in verse 27, *"Now you are the body of Christ, and members
individually."* In order for me to be part of Christ's wife, I must
understand that I cannot personally be the whole body of Christ; I
am only a member of it. Every person must be associated and identified in spirit with the house of God if we are to experience the
fullness that was in Christ. As I rightly relate to others and as I con-
tribute my personal expression of ministry, the church will be
edified, built up and achieve success.

WARNING AGAINST DECEIVERS

We have many warnings against the deceivers that will come including false apostles, prophets, false teachers, false shepherds, false brethren and false christs or anointed ones. You cannot help but understand that this is a serious problem if you are a wise shepherd. The Scriptures say in II Timothy 3:13, *"But evil men and impostors will grow worse and worse, deceiving and being deceived."*

You may think that because you've dealt with something once that it is over and done with. The Holy Spirit says, "And the deceivers shall wax worse and worse." Get back on guard and stay at your post! Things have a way of coming back around. It is like the weeds in your garden. You do not weed once and never have to go back and do it again. As leaders we must maintain constant vigilance.

My former tendency was to let everything go because I thought the Holy Ghost might be in it. I did not want to be guilty of "quenching the Holy Ghost." As a pastor you have to take that chance. Why are you there? You are the watchman! When someone rolls down the aisle, help him out of the meeting and let him roll in an adjacent room. Oh, but it might be God! Oh, but it might not be too!

TRUTH AND HERESY

Let me make this statement, "Error is truth out of balance." Understanding this is so important. Not understanding this is what hurts churches. When truth is out of balance, damage inevitably results. Paul said, I declared to you "the whole counsel of God" (Acts 20:27).

In my earlier days I pastored a church with a "one string banjo", that is, I had one main message—healing and deliverance. It was a good string too. Twang! Twang! Twang! Put it with some other strings and it was great. I preached deliverance, healing, faith, and casting out the devil.

I am not putting that message down. I was raised on that. We pray for the sick all the time. But how many like tacos for every meal they have, or even steak? I tried a steak diet where you only ate steak and they guaranteed weight loss. I ate steak in the morning. I remember my little kids sitting around the table having their porridge and Dad's having this sizzling steak. Dad's on a diet. I ate steak at noon. I ate steak at night. The next morning I ate steak. At noon, I ate steak. After three days I said to my wife, "Honey, is this the same batch of steak you bought when we started this regimen?" It didn't taste the same anymore.

Now I know why you lose weight on the steak diet. After three days it turns into leather in your mouth. I don't care what the truth is. I don't care how wonderful or dynamic it is. One message alone will not build the House of God. You've got to teach the whole counsel. Jesus said it this way, "Teaching them to observe all things that I have commanded you" (Matthew 28:20). This not only includes Jesus words to His disciples, but it includes His words to us in His book—the Bible. "All Scripture is given by inspiration of God, and is profitable for doctrine, for reproof, for correction, for instruction in righteousness, that the man of God may be complete, thoroughly equipped for every good work" (II Tim. 3:16-17). God took such pains to preserve this Book for us so that we could preach a balanced message. A balanced doctrine consists of all that the Bible has to say on that particular subject. A balanced presentation of doctrine includes all of the doctrines of the Bible not just our favorites or the ones that "preach well." And so, error is truth out of balance.

Heresy is mixture. That is my definition. Every heresy has some truth in it and that is why you get hooked into it; it sounds so good. You can look at any of the cults. You can look at the Mormons. Did you know that they believe in speaking in tongues? They believe in apostles and prophets. They believe in eldership management. Yes, they believe and have some restoration teaching that is parallel to much of our teaching. They see themselves as the last day church— the latter day saints. But the truth is they serve another God of their own making. They do not know Jesus as the son of God. As a result they still need a savior.

Many ministries that are in the church world today have an aspect of truth to what they are saying. However, their "truth" taken by itself without the balance of the rest of the Scriptures can lead people astray just as surely as if they taught a fable. Every "new revelation" must be brought into proper context if it is going to produce life. The pastor is the one who is given the challenge to guard the flock from heresy.

CHAPTER TEN

IDENTIFYING
FALSE MINISTRIES

n this chapter I would like to get real practical. I want to give you nine ways to identify false ministries. Before I do, however, I would like to cite some key verses that will lay a foundation for some of the comments that I would like to make and reinforce the responsibility of shepherds when it comes to protecting the people of God from anything that will damage them.

> "I will set up shepherds over them who will feed them; and they shall fear no more, nor be dismayed, nor shall they be lacking." says the LORD.

The Amplified Bible says, *...neither shall any be missing or lost.* Jeremiah 23:4

How beautiful upon the mountains are the feet of him who brings good news, who proclaims peace, who brings glad tidings of good things, who proclaims salvation, who says to Zion, "Your God reigns!" Your watchmen shall lift up their voices, with their voices they shall sing together; for they shall see eye to eye when the LORD brings back Zion. Isaiah 52:7-8

His watchmen are blind, they are all ignorant; they are all dumb dogs, they cannot bark; sleeping, lying down, loving to slumber. Yes, they are greedy dogs which never have enough. And they are shepherds who cannot understand; they all look to their own way, every one for his own gain, from his own territory. "Come," one says, "I will bring wine, and we will fill ourselves with intoxicating drink; tomorrow will be as today, and much more abundant." Isaiah 56:10-12

Son of man, prophesy against the shepherds of Israel, prophesy and say to them, "Thus says the Lord GOD to the shepherds: 'Woe to the shepherds of Israel who feed themselves! Should not the shepherds feed the flocks?'" Ezekiel 34:2

IDENTIFYING FALSE MINISTRY

What are the signs of false ministries? As a shepherd, what are some of the signals that I can watch for as I seek to alert the people that God has placed under my care? I will give you nine signs that help me when I look at a ministry to evaluate it.

1. **False ministries usually will come in as an "angel of light" claiming to have a special revelation from God.**

> *For such are false apostles, deceitful workers, transforming themselves into apostles of Christ. And no wonder! For Satan himself transforms himself into an angel of light. Therefore it is no great thing if his ministers also transform themselves into ministers of righteousness, whose end will be according to their works.*
>
> 2 Corinthians 11:13-15

Someone once said that Satan is ashamed of the man in the gutter. He is ashamed of him because nobody is going to follow a teaching that leads a man to the gutter. So instead Satan comes as a minister of righteousness, clothed in nice apparel, with a pleasing look and a palatable message.

There isn't any false ministry that will wear a sign that says "I am false." On the contrary, they often do great things, they say what we feel that a true minister should say and they look good to the outside observer. But under it all there is a slight "twist." They may bring in a gospel of works. They may add a feature like the Judaizers did. They may add to or take away from the truth.

These ministers come with a special revelation that God has given them personally and that they have been anointed by God to bring it forth. How ridiculous! Is God trying to conceal truth from His people? No! He has given us everything that we need that pertains to life and godliness. Most of the time this "new revelation" sets these false ministers up to be special mediators of this vital truth. "I have the keys! I will help you through the secret door to this area." It ultimately makes people dependent upon their ministry instead of the Holy Spirit.

2. **False ministries usually attack and criticize the spiritual leadership of the local church.**

> *And He Himself gave some to be apostles, some prophets, some evangelists, and some pastors and teachers, for the equipping of the saints for the work of ministry, for the edifying of the body of Christ, till we all come to the unity of the faith and of the knowledge of the Son of God, to a perfect man, to the measure of the stature of the fullness of Christ.* Ephesians 4:11-13

> *For of this sort are those who creep into households and make captives of gullible women loaded down with sins,*

led away by various lusts, always learning and never able
to come to the knowledge of the truth.

II Timothy 3:6-7

Because these false ministries use their "inside track" to God and their "deeper revelation" to foster their ministry, they often set themselves up against the spiritual leadership and elders of the local church. A sincere follower might ask, "Why doesn't our pastor teach this? Why don't we practice this in our church?" To which the reply will be something like, "Most likely because your leadership is from the old school. They are stuck in their traditions. They are not as open to 'new revelation' as they should be. If they were really in touch with the Holy Spirit, they would be teaching this and they would know that this is indeed of God."

As Paul wrote to Timothy, these are the kinds of people who set up in someone's home. They usually find a disgruntled person who is a little naïve or as Paul says, "gullible," who latches onto their teaching and offers their home for these spiritual encounters. This home becomes their base of operations.

Have you ever heard this? "We're meeting over here and we have a revelation that God has shown us and it's really beyond your pastor. He doesn't quite understand this revelation." It is people creeping into our homes or our cities.

Peter mentions these same type of ministers "who walk according to the flesh in the lust of uncleanness and despise authority.

They are presumptuous, self-willed. They are not afraid to speak evil of dignitaries" (II Pet. 2:10). They are not afraid to set themselves up against pastors, elders and church leaders.

God has a government that He has placed in the local church. Every believer has a certain responsibility to properly relate to that government. The writer to the Hebrews goes so far as to say that believers are to "obey those who rule over you, and be submissive, for they watch out for your souls" (Heb. 13:17).

You say, "But don't you know there are bad pastors?" "Oh yes, I know. There are bad policemen. There are bad governors. So what is the answer? Get rid of them all? Get rid of the parents because there are some bad parents? Get rid of all the policemen because there are bad policemen?" If we followed this line, what would you have? We would have anarchy. The government of God includes civil government in society, domestic government in the family and spiritual government in the local church.

3. False ministries usually have a message of doom and use fear to promote it.

> And the peace of God, which surpasses all understanding,
> will guard your hearts and minds through Christ Jesus.
> Finally, brethren, whatever things are true, whatever
> things are noble, whatever things are just, whatever things
> are pure, whatever things are lovely, whatever things are

of good report, if there is any virtue and if there is any-
thing praiseworthy—meditate on these things. The things
which you learned and received and heard and saw in me,
these do, and the God of peace will be with you.

Philippians 4:7-9

But we have renounced the hidden things of shame, not
walking in craftiness nor handling the word of God deceit-
fully, but by manifestation of the truth commending
ourselves to every man's conscience in the sight of God.

II Corinthians 4:2

Will you speak wickedly for God, and talk deceitfully
for Him?   Job 13:7

There are always people that see the cloud inside of every silver lining. There are people who feed on terror. All you have to do is turn on "Christian TV" to see the doomsday prophets. I actually think that some people were really sad that Y2K didn't end the world. Now, I did put a few extra cans of stuff in the cupboards. But I don't live in fear. And, hopefully, I do not use fear to motivate people to serve God.

A few years ago there was a group of over 200 individuals who went into the jungles of Brazil to set up a "wilderness camp." They had a particular interpretation of the Book of Revelation and the man-child company that said that the world was going to be destroyed, but God was going to preserve His people in "the wilderness." They of course believed that they were the "man-child company" that God would want to preserve. So to help God with His plan they were setting up these "wilderness camps" in remote places so that after calamity came upon the earth and when the "dust settled" they would march out of the wilderness and repopulate the earth with a righteous seed.

Do you think that these people were sincere? Tell me, would you go down to the jungle and live a poverty existence if you weren't sincere?

During the time when these camps were operating I was down in Brazil ministering at a leader's conference. At this conference I ran across this man who had just come out of a wilderness camp. I was curious, so I asked him why he came out.

He began to share his experience. He said that everything went well in the camp for about two years. They were quite busy clearing the land, building their little houses and getting in their crops in so that they would have food to eat. Then one day somebody stole something. Since they were the "elect company" they could not have "sin in the camp." Therefore they needed to find out who had done it. They questioned everybody until they finally identified the offender.

I asked this man what they did with the perpetrator. He said that they had to isolate him for awhile until he got cleaned up and until they felt he had experienced true repentance and restoration to purity.

He went on to say that it wasn't but just a few weeks later that two guys were out in the field working and they got into a fist fight. They were slugging each other and had to be pulled apart. He said that this second incident got him to thinking, "This was no different than it was at home!" So much for the man-child company! I am sure that God was extremely disappointed as well.

I call it survival mentality and you're going to hear a lot of it. It will keep coming. It always has and it always will. It is one of Satan's hooks to take you away from the mainstream of God's purpose. Someone is always out there ready to scare you about the future. They are usually just as ready to offer some unbiblical solutions to escape from the imminent doom ahead.

Did Jesus say that when you see the signs of the end times that we should "go into the wilderness?" No! Did he say that when you see these things come to pass "hide under the bed?" No! Jesus said "Lift up your head, rise and shine your light has come." It's harvest time! Harvest is at the end of the world; not the rapture. The harvest is at the end. We're in harvest time. This is not a time to be governed by fear. It is a time to reach out, look up and be encouraged!

4. **False prophets and deceivers usually claim that they have been sent to you by God as His special messenger and usually come from a distant place.**

> *And this occurred because of false brethren secretly brought in (who came in by stealth to spy out our liberty*

which we have in Christ Jesus, that they might bring us into bondage).   Galatians 2:4

Cursed is he who does the work of the LORD deceitfully, and cursed is he who keeps back his sword from blood.

Jeremiah 48:10

For those who are such do not serve our Lord Jesus Christ, but their own belly, and by smooth words and flattering speech deceive the hearts of the simple.

Romans 16:18

This is important. I had a man come into our church one day after I had finally had my core values in place. He proudly announced his arrival, "I'm Apostle Greene from Canada." I had never seen him before and I had never even heard of him. "God sent me here pastor. I've got a word and I'll be speaking here tonight," he added.

I replied, "Well, I'll pray about it." "You don't have to pray about it," he insisted. "Well then, I'll consider it," I said, trying to get him to slow down. But he was quite persistent. "You don't have to consider it. God sent me and I'll be speaking tonight."

That night I got two of the biggest ushers that I had. I told them, "See that guy over there. If he stands up, take him out." Fortunately, the man did not stand up and I guarantee you that he did not speak.

As a pastor, I understand that I am responsible for the flock. I am not just interested in any pulpit supply. When I have a minister in the pulpit, I want to know who they are, where they come from, who they answer to and what do they have to say that this congregation of people needs to hear.

Outside ministers have no right to usurp authority over local leaders. They do not announce their coming as if they were a modern day "John the Baptist." Just because someone touts themselves as an apostle or prophet, it does not mean that local leadership is just to "roll over." No! Never! The traveling ministry should be there to support, uphold and reinforce the authority within the house.

5. False ministries usually have a rebellious, unteachable spirit and will recognize no authority over them.

> *And especially those who walk according to the flesh in the lust of uncleanness and despise authority. They are presumptuous, self-willed. They are not afraid to speak evil of dignitaries.* II Peter 2:10

> *For there are many insubordinate, both idle talkers and deceivers, especially those of the circumcision, whose mouths must be stopped, who subvert whole households, teaching things which they ought not, for the sake of dishonest gain.* Titus 1:10-11

For there are many rebellious people, mere talkers and deceivers, especially those of the circumcision group. They must be silenced, because they are ruining whole households by teaching things they ought not to teach— and that for the sake of dishonest gain. Even one of their own prophets has said, "Cretans are always liars, evil brutes, lazy gluttons." This testimony is true. Therefore, rebuke them sharply, so that they will be sound in the faith and will pay no attention to Jewish myths or to the commands of those who reject the truth. To the pure, all things are pure, but to those who are corrupted and do not believe, nothing is pure. In fact, both their minds and consciences are corrupted. They claim to know God, but by their actions they deny him. They are detestable, disobedient and unfit for doing anything good. Titus 1:10-16 (NIV)

When people would come to me in the past I had several ways to handle them. "God has sent me to you pastor and has put you on my heart and I want to hold you a revival." I would usually say to them, "Where is your home church?" I have had someone say, "Hey, I'm an evangelist. I'm on the road all the time." I would continue to probe, "Where do you hang your hat when you are not preaching?" "At the closest motel." Red flag!

I would continue, "Well, what happens if you run off with the

organist? How do we stop you for your sake?" "What are you saying? I'm a man of God. I would never do something like that!" I
persisted, "Well, it does happen, you know. I am not saying that
you are not a man of God, but we all need covering. If it did happen to you, who would I call to initiate discipline in your life? To
whom do you answer spiritually and financially? To whom do you
give an account?"

Often times I find that they have no real covering for their ministry. They may claim some connection to a small church in the
middle of Kentucky, but they have no tangible connection to the
work, they rarely attend services at the church and they have no
real accountability to its leadership team. The often see themselves
and their ministry as being bigger than the local church.

Sometimes when dealing with such a ministry I will set them
up. I say, "You know, we all need a lot of money for all of our travel
expenses and the orphans that we take care of, so how much
money do you need?" He thinks this is his big chance with such an
understanding minister, "I'll usually need to have about five grand
a weekend." Another red flag! If they set a fee for their services or
ask for money they will not come into our church. The Bible refers
to those who "by covetousness…exploit you with deceptive words"
(II Pet. 2:3).

Don't misinterpret what I am saying. I do believe that the
laborer is worthy of his hire. I do believe you should treat visiting ministry with a liberal spirit. What I am warning you about

is those that do what they do for money and do not have a true shepherd's heart for the people of God.

6. False ministries and deceivers will have the gifts of the Spirit in operation without the corresponding demonstration of the fruit of the Spirit.

> *For false christs and false prophets will rise and show great signs and wonders to deceive, if possible, even the elect.*
>
> Matthew 24:24

> *Put on the full armor of God so that you can take your stand against the devil's schemes. For we are not wrestling with flesh and blood—contending only with physical opponents—but against the despotisms, against the powers against (the master spirits who are) the world rulers of this present darkness, against the spirit forces of wickedness in the heavenly (supernatural) sphere.*
>
> Ephesians 6:11-12 (AMP)

I have always said when you are evaluating ministries, "Put your emphasis on the fruit of the Spirit, not the gifts of the Spirit." The gifts are given to us freely. We do not earn them or deserve them. God gives them to individuals as part of the package that corresponds with their ministry calling in the body of Christ.

Character, on the other hand, is something that grows in our life as we submit to the work of the Holy Spirit in our lives. It is tragically possible to be extremely "gifted" but lack the character of Christ to bring the needed balance to our gift. If the character of a ministry is not in place, they are going to hurt you badly.

I can tell you by experience they are going to hurt you. You know, the problem is this. As it says in Matthew 24:24, "false christs and false prophets will arise and show great signs and wonders to deceive, if possible, even the elect." False ministries at times function with great gifts and powerful anointings. That is a serious problem.

Whenever you bring a "gifted" ministry into your church, I don't care whoever he or she is (he or she could be an incarnation of the devil), he will become somebody's hero. That is the way it is. You want your people to identify with the ministry that you bring in. So, if you bring in false ministries and after they minister freely in your pulpit you have to get up and correct the message by saying something like, "We do not agree with what this ministry said about such and such." You are in trouble.

The people who have been listening to this ministry have had an unfiltered openness to him because they trust you. They trust that if you have this ministry in your pulpit that you have screened him and you are blessing this ministry. There is a strong chance that some people will "buy into" what is being said and all of your disclaimers at the end will not erase the damage that has been done.

I have seen it happen. You make the necessary correction. The people who "bought in" are now offended. They will either cause division in the church or they will end up going somewhere where this ministry is more accepted. You will lose families over these situations.

It is a powerful thing when someone operates in a sign gift. If someone calls out people by name there are people who will believe anything that they say. This was a problem in William Branham's ministry. Because people were healed instantly through his ministry, people thought that the signs were a confirmation that whatever he said was true. And yet, he taught many things that were simply unbiblical. The gift was real, but it was not a verification of his message.

As far as I am concerned I am more careful with ministries when I know that they have a supernatural gifting. They are wonderful but if they do not possess the character of Christ, they can hurt your work more than any other ministry.

7. **False ministries drift in and out of congregations, they have no roots, no spiritual ties, no affiliation with a local church, no pastor who can vouch for them, no reputation that can be verified.**

> *For false christs and false prophets will rise and show great signs and wonders to deceive, if possible, even the elect. "See, I have told you beforehand." Therefore if they say to you, "Look, He is in the desert!" do not go out; or "Look, He is in the inner rooms!" do not believe it.*
>
> Matthew 24:24-26

Jesus warned us because He knew this was going to be a problem and he wants watchmen to be aware. The church is the body of Jesus. It is the Lord's house. He is very jealous over His house. You see, in His House He has provided all that we need. Psalm 23 is a reflection of what is available to us as we remain rightly related to Him and His true shepherds. There is no lack, there is healing, there is provision, there is green pasture, there is discipline and correction and there is abundance. There is really no need to go anywhere else.

There are those who would say, "Come aside with us to the secret chamber." Some times they may be referring to a healing chamber, or special prayer chamber or a discipleship chamber. But all of these things are to be found in the local church. You don't have to go into the desert. You don't have to go into a cave or a secret chamber. All of this has been provided in the place of God's choosing, the local church. And if a particular local church is not such a place our efforts should be focused on adorning the local church with these functions.

Now, I know I am touching on some touchy things here, but if you want things to get out of control then just let anything go. Unfortunately, the secret chamber ministries do not have biblical structure and accountability. In fact, their tendency is to drain the local church of its strength by promising some special blessing to those who support the secret chamber ministry.

We had a lady who was sick several years ago. She received a call from some well meaning people saying she should come to the desert in Arizona and get healed down there. There was a special group that felt that they had the key for healing. She came to me and said she really thought she should go down there. "They are getting healed down there in the desert."

As she was speaking to me this scripture came into mind, *Therefore if they say to you, "Look, He is in the desert!" do not go out; or "Look, He is in the inner rooms!" do not believe it.* So I said to her, "You don't need to go anywhere. We will pray for you here. We will minister to you here." "No, I want to go down there. They just really say there are supernatural miracles there," she insisted.

The sad part of the story is that she did go down to the desert. Unfortunately, things did not work out well for her. In fact, she died in the desert, alone.

When Jesus warned us about this scenario, He didn't say it casually. He is building his church! The local church is the place of His provision. We've got to have faith in our churches for healing. We move into danger when we separate any ministry from the House of God.

8. False ministries have a love of money, a covetous spirit.

> *By covetousness they will exploit you with deceptive words;*
> *for a long time their judgment has not been idle, and their*
> *destruction does not slumber.*   II Peter 2:3

*And through covetousness shall they with feigned words
make merchandise of you: whose judgment now of a long
time lingereth not, and their damnation slumbereth not.*

2 Peter 2:3 (KJV)

I've been in places and heard ministries say, "If you want a $20 prophecy, come up. If you want a $100 prophecy you come over here." It is so sad that often the "bigger" a ministry gets the more demanding that they become. They demand to be treated a certain way. They demand a certain amount of money if they are to come. They must stay in a five-star hotel.

But ever sadder is that we put up with this. Perhaps the saddest scripture in the whole Bible is Jeremiah 5:31. Please make note of it, *And the prophets prophecy falsely, and the priests bear rule by their means. And my people love to have it so* (KJV). My people love it that way! They love false prophecy. They don't mind being ripped off financially? Why? Because they get the goose bumps. They like the excitement. They like the things that are going to cause their emotions to be aroused. "Ooooooh, did you feel that?" We don't care if the prophecy is false; it excited us at the moment. The prophecy was an end in itself.

As pastors and leaders, however, we must care. False prophecy will not produce edification and maturity in the people. We are watchmen, shepherds and overseers. We are to guard the Body of Christ.

9. **False ministries and deceivers have little respect for the local church and local church government (eldership).**

> *I will build my church, and the gates of Hades shall not prevail against it.*   Matthew 16:18

> *But Christ as a Son over His own house, whose house we are if we hold fast the confidence and the rejoicing of the hope firm to the end.*   Hebrews 3:6

> *For we are members of His body, of His flesh and of His bones. "For this reason a man shall leave his father and mother and be joined to his wife, and the two shall become one flesh." This is a great mystery, but I speak concerning Christ and the church.*   Ephesians 5:30-32 (KJV)

I had a very interesting experience several years ago in which I had the privilege of receiving a number of copies of the Sharon Star, which was the publication of the 1948 Latter Rain movement. This magazine reported to the world what was going on during that particular outpouring of the Holy Spirit.

If you know anything about Latter Rain there was a true move of the Holy Spirit and a number of truths that we enjoy today really came out of the Latter Rain move, such as extended free worship in song and praise and the laying on of hands and prophecy. The problem was that Latter Rain became "scatter rain." It actually became a movement that divided and destroyed many churches and though there was an original true outpouring of the Spirit, it ended in frustration and division in the body of Christ.

These Sharon Stars—about 15 altogether—were printed in that period of time. My wife attended the Bible College in North Battleford in 1949 and I had an interest as to what really took place during the Latter Rain outpouring. I read through all of these magazines to try and understand what they actually taught during the original outpouring. I soon discovered why Latter Rain became "scatter rain."

As I read with anticipation, I soon realized that in all that they taught about the moving of the Holy Spirit and the restoration of prophetic ministries, there was absolutely no emphasis on the local church and local church government. The entire focus was on the universal church and how those who were being touched by God needed to come out of our ditches (i.e. local churches) in order to be part of the latter rain outpouring.

It is not hard to see why so many of these prophets and five-fold ministers could go into churches and literally destroy some of them because there was no respect for the autonomy and the sovereignty of the local church. Not one article was about church government. It is quite obvious that if you take away government you have anarchy. That is exactly what came out of the Latter Rain movement because there was imbalance concerning the House of God.

My closing statement is this. If you want to protect the church from false ministries that the enemy would use to destroy the church, you must make sure that all of the ministries that stand before the people have based their ministry on the local church. By that I mean, they are local church minded apostles, prophets, pastors, teachers and evangelists. They have one thing in mind and that is to build what Jesus is building—the local church.